THE CYBER PIMP

What Every Parent
Should Know to
Safeguard
Their Children from
Online Sex Predators

Moneé Brown MA, BS

LDM
Leadership DevelopME, LLC
Publishing Services

TABLE OF CONTENTS

DEDICATION

Marty (brother) and Jacquelyn (BFF), whose presence in my life was a true gift. Though you have left this world, your memory and the impact you two made on my life will forever be cherished. This dedication stands as a tribute to the love we shared, the memories we created, and the lessons you taught me. Your passing may have left a void in my heart, but it also serves as a reminder to cherish every moment and embrace the beauty of life. Thank you for the precious moments and the love we shared. This dedication is a testament to your profound impact on my life and the eternal love that binds us, transcending the boundaries of time and space. My forever guardian angels!

To my beloved grandmother, Delores, this book is dedicated to you, my guiding light, my source of encouragement, and the person who instilled in me the value of education. Although you are no longer with us, your memory and impact on my life will forever shine brightly. This dedication is a tribute to your enduring support, profound wisdom, and the love you showered upon me. Your belief in my potential, even during moments of self-doubt, inspired me to overcome obstacles and reach for the stars. I am forever grateful for the love and guidance you shared.

To the best mother in the world, Donna, I couldn't have done it without you. This book is dedicated to you, my guiding light, my source of unconditional love, and my forever inspiration. Throughout my life, you have shown me what it means to be strong, compassionate, forgiving, and resilient. Your resolute support has been a constant source of comfort and encouragement. This dedication serves as a humble tribute to the countless sacrifices you have made, the sleepless nights you endured, and the belief you have had in my dreams. Your belief in my potential has fueled my creative fire. Thank you for being more than a mother - a confidante, a cheerleader, and a source of wisdom. Your love has shaped me into the person I am today, and I am eternally grateful for your presence in my life.

To my dad, Tyrone, thank you for all your support, boundless wisdom, and encouraging words along this journey. To Anita, my guiding light, my source of strength, and a pillar of love throughout my life. Your nurturing presence and boundless support have shaped me into the person I am today. Like a mother, you have been through the ups and downs, the triumphs and challenges, offering a listening ear and words of wisdom. Your unconditional love has provided comfort and encouragement in every step of my journey. Thank you for being a source of endless love and inspiration in my life. I am eternally grateful.

Ira, you are the best little brother, my rock, my partner in crime, and my relentless support. From the very beginning, you have been by my side, cheering me on and believing in my dreams. Your encouragement and love have been a driving force behind my journey.

To my uncle Dennis (dad) and Auntie Pat (mom), my surrogate parents, this book is dedicated to the two extraordinary souls who have embraced me with open arms, providing steadfast love, guidance, and a sense of belonging. From the moment we crossed paths, 48 years ago, you have filled my life with warmth, understanding, and endless support. In your presence, I have found a second home - a sanctuary where I am accepted for who I am and where my dreams are nurtured with boundless encouragement. Your parental love has been a source of strength and inspiration throughout the journey of this book. Your anchoring belief in my potential has fueled my determination and propelled me forward. This dedication is a tribute to your immeasurable impact on my life. Your love and guidance have shaped me into who I am today, and I am forever grateful for your role as my surrogate parents.

To my children, Tiara, Lauren, and Jordyn thank you for inspiring me to keep working hard when I wanted to give up. Lauren, thanks for giving me permission to share with others so we can inform other parents and youth of the pitfalls of electronic devices and the internet.

My sister/BFF, Marie, this book is dedicated to you, my steadfast companion and confidante. From the very beginning of our journey together, you have been my rock, my source of laughter, and a constant source of inspiration. Your support and belief in me have been a guiding light through the creative process of this book. Your friendship has taught me the true meaning of loyalty, and I am forever grateful for your presence in my life. Your support and encouragement are priceless; everyone "deserves a sister like Marie."

To my girl, Bea, thank you for your endless friendship, patience, and guidance. Your belief in my potential and support propelled me forward, even when I faced challenges. This book reflects the remarkable journey we shared and the gratitude I hold in my heart for your invaluable presence in my life. You are one in a million.

To my sisters Shonta, Stefanie, Roz, and Helen, my pillars of support, laughter partners, and kindred spirits. Through the highs and lows, you've been there with love and encouragement. Your sistership has been a constant source of inspiration and strength. Your belief in me and ability to lift my spirits have fueled my drive to complete this book. Through the power of our sistership, we've shared countless memories, laughter, and even tears. May this book serve as a tribute to our unbreakable bond and the extraordinary adventures we've embarked on together and the one's to come.

Amena, Amanda, Kimberley, Monty, Keandra, Shon, and Kishia, this book is dedicated to you, my cherished cousins who are more like siblings to me. Through the twists and turns of life, you have always been there, offering support, laughter, and a bond that knows no bounds. This dedication is a tribute to our love, friendship, and sisterhood. From childhood adventures to late-night conversations filled with dreams and aspirations, you have been my pillars of strength and a constant source of inspiration. Thank you for the laughter, the shared secrets, and the support that has carried me through the highs and lows. Together, we have created a tapestry of memories that will forever hold a special place in my heart.

Aaron, my husband, my partner in love and life, and my best friend, you are my source of support. Since our paths crossed, you have filled my world with boundless love, joy, and inspiration. In the pages of this book, as I weave stories of love, resilience, and growth, I am reminded of your profound impact on my life. Your belief in my dreams and your constant encouragement have been the driving force behind my creative journey. This dedication is a testament to our deep connection, the adventures we have embarked upon together, and the love that binds us. Your presence by my side has brought light to even the darkest moments, and your support has given me the courage to chase my dreams. Thank you for being my rock, confidant, and biggest cheerleader. Your love has been a constant source of strength and inspiration, and I am eternally grateful for the warmth and security you bring to our lives.

May this book serve as a reminder of the love we share and the beautiful journey we continue to embark upon together. With you by my side, every chapter of our lives becomes a remarkable adventure.

WHY THIS BOOK?

Parents, family members, and communities are concerned about identifying the risks of children's harmful online interactions. You might wonder how to avoid your loved ones becoming damaged by fraud and predators online. At the extremes, children can become involved in exploitation, including sex trafficking. Young people growing up in the Internet age use digital technology and social media as second nature. However, many children and adolescents are naïve and vulnerable to abuse and solicitation online, and in the worst case, by sex traffickers. Over the past 15 years, sexually exploited children have had more frequent contact with abusers online versus call services or public places. In 2015, 75% of youth were trafficked online versus 38% in 2004.[1] The National Center for Missing and Exploited Children found an 846% increase in youth

---

[1] Bouché, V. (2011). Sex trafficking: Inside the business of modern day slavery (review). *Human Rights Quarterly, 33*(3), 899–906.

exploitation through the Internet between 2010 and 2015.[2] These activities increased notably during the pandemic.

Words like grooming and human trafficking are commonly used in society these days to describe what happens with adults and children victimized by online traffickers. But what do these words really mean, and what can we do to prevent, heal, and bring predators to account? I offered a beginning for parents and other stakeholders to understand these issues. I have included some of my stories below so that you can see how many lives have been touched.

Throughout this book, you will also find resources in the text, at the end of the book, and references as footnotes. The resources are for the general public, and references are there for anyone's in-depth reading—some of the resources are linked in the text so that you can directly view websites with information. Also, note that I have backed some information using research findings. I offer them to give you confidence in the information I present. The Internet sometimes contains inaccurate information, and you deserve to know reliable facts from good sources.

Although it is hard to believe, evidence is all around us that Internet predators are stalking and luring children online. This growing problem is exacerbated by some parents' unawareness that

---

[2] Canessa, R (2018). *Interrupting the vicious cycle of online sex trafficking.* Medium. Equality Now. https://equalitynow.medium.com/interrupting-the-vicious-cycle-of-online-sex-trafficking-f1821d737221e

sex traffickers are soliciting, grooming, and exploiting youth at alarming rates via online platforms, such as chatrooms, discussion rooms, bulletin boards, emails, and social networking sites.[34] All stakeholders, especially parents, need more information about how Internet predators find and connect with their kids, what comprises sexual exploitation and predation, how children are drawn into it, the risks and signs, and the outcomes. Information about the problem can be invaluable to all concerned, but many people are unaware of the problem and where resources for help and support can be found. For example, lifelines and services are available, such as the National Center for Missing and Exploited Children (https://www.missingkids.org/)[5], but I find that one-to-one parent education and in-person interventions can be crucial before and after families have these unthinkable experiences.

Through this book, I show some hard evidence that sexual predators exist and have access to children, and most crucially, traffickers can pull almost anyone's child into this heinous crime. The parents I mention below attest directly to it. This book aims to help parents identify the factors that could place their children at greater risk of online solicitation, specifically for the most evil, sex

---

[3] Durkin, K. F., & DeLong, R. L. (2018). Internet-facilitated child sexual exploitation crimes. In *Encyclopedia of information science and technology*, 4th ed. (pp. 1366-1375). IGI Global

[4] Reid, J., & Fox, B. (2020). Human trafficking and the darknet: Technology, innovation, and evolving criminal justice strategies. In *Science Informed policing* (pp. 77-96). Springer, Cham.

[5] National Center for Missing and Exploited Children. https://www.missingkids.org/

trafficking. I aim to bring information and facts to parents and others concerning the risks of children's use of digital devices on the Internet and social media and, most of all, how children's online activity can lead to sexual exploitation. After surviving these traumatic experiences, parents and children need to identify the traumatic consequences of sex trafficking. This book contains suggestions about supervision and talking with your children about the dangers of Internet and social media communication with unknown people. Additionally, therapeutic interventions and one specific recovery program for children and families are outlined to demonstrate how these resources can be used. Next, I give some of my story.

BEING GROOMED:
I NEVER THOUGHT IT COULD BE ME

I wrote this book after hearing so many pieces of stories from children, parents, and families about their experiences of sex trafficking and abuse. I added my story because too many of these pieces could have fit into my life. Fortunately, I was not sex-trafficked, but while in high school, I fell under the influence of an older man. I grew up in a different time before the Internet made predators' access to children faster and easier—perhaps that is part of what spared me; our lives did not move as fast back then. The speed with which these predators can move into a child's life is unprecedented, and many of us remain at a loss as to how and when it happens. I will share some of my story, so you know that you are not alone. We all know that although the stories of older generations unfolded differently, they are still relatable across generations and changing times. And they make us that much more aware of how times have changed. Across generations, we can come together to understand the hurt and pain to get better.

I was raised in Oakland, CA, in a loving single-family home. My father was an integral part of my life, but he fell victim to the streets and was in and out of prison. Ultimately, my father's absence left me without a full-time father figure. As I was growing up in the late 1980s and early '90s, my parents' biggest fear was seeing me cross paths with older men, men as much as 10 years older who lurked in the neighborhood seeking girls and young women. Back then, we referred to them as "cat daddies" because they often drove flashy Cadillacs. Even though these predators were more often seen in person than today's cyber-pimps, in those days, parents and kids alike could be unaware of the dangers.

My parents' worst nightmare came to fruition; unbeknownst to them, I began dating an older man during my sophomore year of high school — a cat daddy. He fed into my need for a more consistent presence of a father in my life; this man seemed to fill that void. Dating an older man came with perks such as food, sex, gifts, transportation, money, and love, or so I thought. At my age, I didn't understand that this older man provided what I was missing with my father. I wanted to feel loved, seen, and heard, and this man offered this to me, but it came at a cost. I know now that I became involved with an older man because I had low self-esteem, was insecure, and had been a victim of sexual abuse by my babysitter. My parents were unaware of my feelings and the abuse.; I was too afraid to share it; I blamed myself and felt ashamed. Back then, I would have never realized I was being groomed, but that is precisely what it was.

I still reflect on what someone could have said or done to help me come forward after I met that older man. I was unsure that anyone could have helped me heal from the trauma, even if I had disclosed these abuses. Sadly, on my path to recovery, resources have sometimes seemed limited and hard to find. After meeting so many victimized families, I realize that even in a new and different era, things have not changed much; resources remain limited regarding support for child survivors of sex solicitation and their families, particularly for the more recent means predators use, online sex solicitation.

Reflecting on my childhood, no one would have thought I was suffering emotionally because I appeared to have it all. On the surface, people saw that my family was middle class, and I excelled in high school, graduating at the top of my class. But the reality is that no one ever asked if I was okay. I decided to pursue a bachelor's degree in criminal justice. I wanted to understand why people break the law, but more importantly, explain to offenders how they affect their families — emotionally, physically, and financially.

In 2001, I obtained a Criminal Justice degree and began working as a Juvenile Deputy Probation Officer for the Alameda County Probation Department. I was assigned to work in the Family Preservation Unit, which dealt with youths who had committed heinous crimes. If they failed to abide by their terms and conditions or probation, they would be removed from their home and placed in a group home. The majority of the cases that I had were girls who had been arrested for solicitation. Working with this high-risk population, I began to understand that these young people, girls and boys, from every social background, racial, ethnic group, and sexual/gender identity, had been exploited. Many were initially victimized through the Internet and phone messaging. I realized that children of all ages were solicited through social media. I saw the grief of parents who had given their children the very best they could give, including the latest technology, unknowingly making their kids vulnerable to predators and sex trafficking. Parents provide their kids with digital devices to keep in contact with them; however, it opens a portal for abusers to stay in near-constant contact with the children they stalk and groom and do so clandestinely.

Over the years, parents sometimes confided to me that they did not believe they needed to monitor their children's Internet use and digital devices. If I asked parents outright about checking their youths' devices, many said, "No, I don't have the password," or "I trust my kid." I tried to relay to them that it is seldom about trusting their children but more about not knowing or trusting the people their kids encounter. One parent shared with me, " I did not want my daughter to grow up distrustful of the world, but as I found out, she grew up using the Internet. It's normal for her to be online with friends; she just trusts too quickly." "When you think about it, there is rarely a legitimate reason for an adult to carry on an ongoing relationship with minor children where parents don't know." One told me her daughter "divulged personal information to a predator, such as our names, employers, location, and those of other family members. Worse still, they gained access to our finances." Her voice broke as she said, "it's taken years to sort this out and regain our financial footing." Others elaborated on how the whole family's safety was affected. We received "threatening calls to our house and ended up taking out the line they called on."

As my abuser had done to me years ago, some parents described that predators groomed kids to show loyalty by sharing secrets. My abuser told me my parents "really did not love me, and they would only keep us apart. We should just go off together, just you and me." Years later, as a probation officer, I heard a parent say, "After talking with my child about her abuser, I realized that this stranger was attempting to build a world just for my child and keep her apart from real life."

Sharing a secret allows sex predators to gain trust, uncover the youth's vulnerabilities, and be attentive to their needs. My predator had found my need for a strong male figure who could shower me with attention by offering money and buying clothing, food, and anything he could to make me feel special. Sadly, as I realized in a different era while on my path to recovery, things have not changed much; resources are limited to supporting child survivors of sex solicitation and their families, particularly now in the newest version using online sex solicitation. Children sometimes feel indebted to a predator.

Fortunately, I did not succumb to encouragement to run away from home to be with him, but many others have. Leaving home is often where the tragedies become full-blown horrors. Parents described to me that after returning home, their children had been raped, beaten, and drugged. This torture leads to choices parents would never dream their children could make. To my great astonishment, I learned that many survivors continued to leave home endless times to return to their abusers--they were conditioned. Their parents felt the kids were losing their identities and trust in reality: "I felt I did not know him anymore, but worse than that, he did not seem to know himself anymore." This parent continued, "I withered inside each time it happened. I was losing myself, too, as I watched my child become someone else. You just want to withdraw from the whole world."

As a mother of girls, my heart has always ached for the families that had to endure the pain and sleepless nights of wondering if they would ever see their child alive again or if they were safe. Some children and parents expressed fear that these vivid memories of what happened would never leave them. After everyone I spoke with,

I was filled with dread, knowing that because many survivors rarely give detailed information about predators, they are not stopped. And the cycle continues while they create a new victim.

My experience as a Deputy Probation Officer came with much pain. I witnessed very few positive outcomes and success stories working with these survivors. Sadly, as I realized in a different era while on my path to recovery, things have not changed much; resources are limited in supporting child survivors of sex solicitation and their families, particularly now in the newest version using online sex solicitation.

What the Author Wants You to Know

Electronic devices and the Internet have made it easier for sex predators to pimp, solicit, and groom our children without repercussion. As a mother, my heart aches for any parent who has experienced their child's victimization by online sex solicitation, regardless of the youth's gender, sexual orientation, ethnicity, social/criminal status, or parent's economic status. The clients and I had risk factors (low self-esteem, being bullied, lack of a parental figure, homelessness, gender identity, and mental health) that placed us at higher risk of being solicited and groomed by predators. Suppose a parent is not having an ongoing discussion with their youth about the dos and don'ts of social media, which include monitoring and knowing the passwords to their youth's electronic devices. In that case, there is a high probability that your youth's safety could be at risk. If a parent is willing to provide an electronic device to their youth, they must be willing to talk about sex, sex predators, safety, and social media etiquette before and after providing their youth an electronic device. Once a youth is provided an electronic device, they can research any information through the world wide web using their electronic device to find any information that may or may not be factual without their parent's knowledge.

After reading this book, I hope parents and youth will become educated on the dangers of the Internet. I am asking youth to pledge to "Don't Chat Back" to anyone they do not know via social media using any electronic device. I hope my books "Operation: *Don't Chat Back and Ready, Set, Game!*" will start and continue the dialogue amongst parents, youth, community, law enforcement, social media leaders, and legislation to bring harsher laws to safeguard our children against online sex predators.

PARENTS AS SURVIVORS TOO

Parents often carry guilt and shame concerning the exploitation of their children. *When we think about it, parents can be victims too, but they are also their children's greatest resource for healing.* Using my professional background in the justice system and graduate studies in family interventions, I offer a window into how we can help young survivors and support parents to overcome traumatic experiences related to sex trafficking.

I continue this journey by explaining how the pandemic worsened the problem, how predators operate, and specific risk factors for children and families. It's essential to remember that although some vulnerable groups have far more risks, almost anyone or any family can fall prey to abusers due to their free and open access to Internet users. For starters, I set the stage for how the pandemic has accelerated predator access and made the Internet an even more significant risk factor.

The Pandemic and Internet Use as Increasing the Risks

Like many other social problems, child abuse circumstances changed during the pandemic. People were on lockdown, and often, you may have feared letting children back into the world even after restrictions were loosened. Children could not socialize as much with family, friends, and schoolmates. Because so many more children were at home using online learning, strangers had access to children, and online sex traffickers took advantage to contact, solicit, recruit, and groom youths online without their parent's, schools', and law enforcement's knowledge[6]. The National Center for Missing and Exploited Children backs up the apparent risk increase during the pandemic. They received 4.2 million complaints of online solicitation of children in April 2020, a 2.2 million increase from the previous month just before the pandemic became widespread.[7] Clearly, the pandemic exploded as a risk factor for online exploitation.

Well before the pandemic increased the risks, using the Internet and social media provided abusers with access to children. The problem has grown since the late 1980s; sexual predators have solicited children using various technology platforms without parental knowledge.[8] Although some are more vulnerable to online abuse, almost anyone can be drawn into this evil. Experienced predators know the vulnerabilities of those who will likely fall prey,

---

[6] Reid, J., & Fox, B. (2020).

[7] Brewster, T. (2020). *Online child abuse complaints surpass 4 million in April. This is how cops are coping despite COVID-19.* https://www.forbes.com/sites/thomasbrewster/2020/05/09/online-child-abuse-complaints-surpass-4-million-in-april-this-is-how-cops-are-coping-despite-covid-19/?sh=31faaf6448db

[8] Detrick, S. (1998). Sites launched to combat child sexual exploitation on the Internet. *International Journal of Children's Rights, 6,* 115.

and they seek out those fitting the profile. Finding children to target has become increasingly easier for abusers; estimates are that over 500,000 predators are online every day looking for young people under 18.[9] If youths have one or more risk factors, such as mental health issues, illicit substance use, and family turmoil, they are more easily solicited by a seemingly caring stranger.[10]

Clearly, during and since the pandemic, the problem appears to be spinning out of control. Parents need to understand the realities of how predators can prey on children.

Who are Cyber Pimps and Traffickers?

Many people are shocked that children can be lured into sexual abuse and trafficking as often as they do. Predators can be people known to children and families and appear as upstanding community members; they can be teachers, ministers, principals, coaches, family friends, and shadowy figures participating in social media. Online and face-to-face sexual predators are experts at luring children and gaining their trust. They often appear interested in the child's school,

---

[9] Nelson, P. (2022). *Deep Dive: FBI estimates 500,000 online predators are a daily threat to kids going online. Investigators say predators use multiple platforms.* KOAA News. https://www.koaa.com/news/deep-dive/fbi-estimates-500-000-online-predators-are-a-daily-threat-to-kids-going-online

[10] Franchino-Olsen, H. (2021). Vulnerabilities relevant for commercial sexual exploitation of children/domestic minor sex trafficking: A systematic review of risk factors. *Trauma, Violence, & Abuse, 22*(1), 99-111.

home, personal, and social lives. Some online abusers are known sex offenders in the judicial system.

All these abusers have in common the skills to manipulate people to perform behaviors they would not have without the influence of the abuser. They often make young people believe they are their only friends and encourage kids to give them information about themselves and their families. For example, predators are gifted at getting impressionable youths to offer personal information rather quickly, even within the first week of conversing with the predator.[11] While some cyber pimps are pedophilic abusers operating in isolation, and others are not necessarily compulsive sexual abusers but are profiteers of the most vulnerable in our society.

Organized sex traffickers are business people. Many people may not be aware that sex trafficking is the third most lucrative offense after narcotics and firearms.[12] Surprising for some of us is that sex traffickers worldwide make a yearly average profit of $21,800 per sex-trafficked victim.[13] Nevertheless, other criminal endeavors are also profitable too, such as human labor or drug trafficking. Why are individuals and criminal enterprises drawn to human trafficking

---

[11] Brewster (2020),

[12] Deshpande, N. A., & Nour, N. M. (2013). Sex trafficking of women and girls. *Reviews in Obstetrics and Gynecology, 6*(1), e22.

[13] Kar, D., & Spanjers, J. (2017). *Transnational crime and the developing world.* Global Financial Integrity..

versus other illegal profiteering? Let's start with an example we can use throughout the book. A strategy used by adult predators is to create a dependent relationship by offering drugs to those they victimize.[14] Some might wonder, if these predators can access illicit drugs, why not sell drugs rather than people? As Jennifer Swain of Youth Smart said, "You can sell a bag of drugs once, but you can sell a person multiple time[s]"[15]

Easy access to young survivors on the Internet and through smartphones has exploded the opportunities for these criminals to profit. About 88% of youth between the ages of 13 to17 have access to the Internet through mobile devices. Approximately three-quarters of youths own a smartphone, 30% have a basic phone, and only 12% do not have a mobile device.[16] Children's frequent usage creates access for predators — 92% of youth search the Internet at least once daily, and 24% surf the Internet continuously. In addition, 71% of youths between the ages of 13 to 17 use Facebook, 52% use Instagram, 41% use Snapchat, and 33% use Twitter. Clearly, kids are spending much

[14] U.S. Department of Health and Human Services. (n.d.). *Resources: Common health issues seen in victims of Human trafficking.* https://www.acf.hhs.gov/sites/default/files/documents/orr/health_problems_seen_in_traffick_victims.pdf

[15] Olsen, E. (2021). *Human trafficking: Global threat to fundamental human rights.* Global Peace Foundation. https://globalpeace.org/human-trafficking-global-threat-to-fundamental-human-rights/

[16] Anderson, M., & Jiang, J. (2018). Teens, social media & technology 2018. *Pew Research Center, 31*(2018), 1673-1689; Lenhart, A. (2015). *Teens, social media & technology overview 2015.*Pew Research Center. https://www.pewresearch.org/internet/2015/04/09/teens-social-media-technology-2015/.

of their time online, and predators are savvy at finding these young people using their tools of the trade and exploiting kids during daily social media use.

As described below, human trafficking stands apart from most forms of sexual and physical abuse. Once in the hands of commercial sex predators, many children are exposed to sex, drugs, alcohol, and the worst cases, raped and physically, mentally, and emotionally tormented. These predators use methods referred to as grooming, among other tactics. I want to help you better understand how these abusers operate. Making the tactics and outcomes understandable to the public is a first step toward action and prevention. You also need to know more about what these predators do and how they do it.

As described below, human trafficking stands apart from most forms of sexual and physical abuse. These predators use methods referred to as grooming, among other methods. I will now help you better understand how these abusers operate.

What is Human Trafficking, and How is it Linked to Grooming?

Personally, I do not believe it's too dramatic to describe human trafficking as modern-day slavery. O'Brien and colleagues defined sex trafficking of young people as an exchange of something of value for forced sexual activity involving a child.[17] Human trafficking is about forcing victims into sex acts using fraud and coercion. It is a worldwide phenomenon that includes adults and children. The enslaved people are forced into labor or involuntary servitude, as described historically in all forms of slavery. These victims are often held captive or in servitude by debt bondage or forcing them to use their bodies to pay off someone's debts.[18]

Commercial sex trafficking, including prostitution, operates on circumstances such as making the victims addicted to substances and holding them under debt bondage. Sometimes threats of harm to family members and the children's lives keep the victims with these pimps. Offering drugs and threatening kids are stages of grooming, as described in the next section.[19] Some of these details are more than distasteful, but I believe parents should know what they are dealing with.

What is grooming, and How Does it Happen in Stages?

First, we might all think we know what grooming is, but let's ensure you fully grasp it. Grooming is often heard in popular culture

---

[17] O'Brien, J., Finkelhor, D., & Jones, L. (2022). Improving services for youth survivors of commercial sexual exploitation: Insights from interventions with other high-risk youth. *Children and Youth Services Review, 132*, 106313.

[18] U.S. Department of State. (n.d.). *What is modern day slavery? Sex trafficking.* https://www.state.gov/what-is-modern-slavery

[19] U.S. Department of State. (n.d.). https://www.state.gov/what-is-modern-slavery

and used by psychologists; however, many adults are not well-versed in how it can happen. Parents need to know what grooming can look like.

As described throughout this book, the biggest commonality among child predators and abusers is grooming victims to gain trust and form a relationship with the intent to abuse and/or traffic children for commercial sex.[20] Sexual predators have common strategies and patterns to draw kids into relationships. Grooming takes time, and there are red flags for parents as it progresses. Understanding the mindset of these criminals can give parents added insights into how to avoid them and when they may be lurking. Psychologists tell us that groomers are methodical[21]. Although every case can differ, they often take similar steps in procuring victims (https://www.webmd.com/sex/what-is-sexual-grooming).[22] Knowing their steps can make you much more savvy about helping your children and their teachers understand how to prevent it. Parents, teachers, and the whole community must know the signals to implement prevention.

---

[20] Sreenivas, S. (2022). *What Is Sexual Grooming?* WebMD. https://www.webmd.com/sex/what-is-sexual-grooming

[21] O'Brien, J. E., & Li, W. (2020). The role of the Internet in the grooming, exploitation, and exit of United States domestic minor sex trafficking victims. *Journal of Children and Media, 14*(2), 187-203.

[22] Sreenivas (2022).

I have used some specific examples to understand the signs of grooming and the steps predators use to procure victims. Although these methods and signs are similar for trafficked adults and children, the frame of reference is mostly for child victims. As detailed in steps 1 to 4, the early signs of grooming are pivotal to notice so that parents can become aware before it's too late. Discussion points 5 and 6 continue with the advanced stages of grooming and trafficking.

First, let's review the steps abusers take, then go through some red flags for parents.

- **Step 1: Choosing a Victim.** An in-person or online groomer observes potential victims by watching or listening to them for a while. For example, children engaged with online social media may be chosen firstly for ease of access to them. Children often project who they are; they have not yet learned the adult masks we use to defend our egos against harm. For example, groomers look for children who mention their parents, and other adults are often not around. They also look for victims who seem guileless about needing a friend.

- **Step 2: Increasing Access and Starting to Build False Trust.** Predators know how to strike up a conversation with kids quickly. They can be charming and friendly, lowering young people's alertness about what they say and do. They are looking to have children let down their guard and become engaged.

- **Step 3: Continuing to Build Trust.** Once they have access and lower a child's guard, they show unexpected generosity, such as praising children or luring them into playing online games. Eventually, they want to capture attention using one-on-one time in chat rooms or digital messaging. Furthermore, sexual predators lure underaged victims with a promise to love and accept them unconditionally and/or provide for their physical well-being[23]. Gift-giving often begins and increases in this phase, along with sharing secrets that can make kids feel special and safe.

- **Step 4: Isolating the Victim.** Predators gain youths' trust by finding ways to come between children and their families and friends. They are experts at distracting kids' attention from people close to them. Isolating children builds a world where they think they have an unfailing friend and little need for everything else. The predator becomes a go-to person for anything.

- **Step 5: Normalizing the Relationship.** Online approaches to children obviously limit how a predator can normalize sexual behavior in a child. However, as we know, the Internet is full of adult sexual references, visual content, and conversations.

---

[23] Kaylor, L. (2015). *Psychological impact of human trafficking and sex slavery worldwide: Empowerment and intervention.* John Jay College of Criminal Justice New York.

Introducing children to ways of finding and using sexual content is an important step for cyber predators to succeed. Also, if a perpetrator can help children obtain drugs or alcohol, these substances lower inhibitions and lure kids into watching porn and other sexual content. These children can become less fearful when taking drugs or alcohol. Online abusers can show children videos and pictures to make everything seem normal, including telling sexual jokes, and encourage keeping these things a secret just between the two of them.

People often masquerade as imposters, using fake names and backgrounds to engage with others. These fake personas are often perpetrated on adults in dating forums online, but the game is the same when enticing children. These methods are often called "catfishing" to get people interested and show interest in others for fraudulent or nefarious purposes. Social media sites can be hazardous for catfishing kids. [24]

- **Step 6: Maintain Control and Power.** At this phase, abuse and trafficking ensue, but first, a predator must exercise control over their targets to increase their chances of success and decrease their chances of being caught. This step deserves

---

[24] Catfishing. (2023, June 21). In *Wikipedia*. https://en.wikipedia.org/wiki/Catfishing

much detail, and I have given it below; work through it because it's disturbing but valuable information.

Gaining control is a crucial step. After sex traffickers have access and direct contact, they often threaten or use mental and physical violence to gain control of the relationship.[25] Control is often executed by choosing children who are already vulnerable and even making them less vulnerable, more so by making threats against their families and/or creating indebtedness situations. At this stage, the predator works to open the door to blackmailing kids for sex. Statistics show that to reach this control stage, 64% of sex traffickers communicate with their victims for at least a month, but a month is not enough time, and changes in children can go unnoticed by those around them.

Sexual normalization can occur through several routes, even using online methods. Seventy-nine percent of perpetrators communicated with victims using an electronic device, 48% sent pictures of themselves, sometimes nude, and 47% sent sexually oriented gifts without the parents' knowledge. Collective data from various law enforcement agencies shows that about 54% of youths who were sexually exploited met their

---

[25] Kaylor (2015)

predators online, 26% through call service, and 9% in a public place[26]. Thus, the majority are currently finding their victims online initially.

Once groomers have mastered control, emotional closeness becomes their tool to manipulate kids, but fear is their greatest weapon in maintaining the relationship. Children who have become emotionally dependent on predators may feel rejection if the perpetrator threatens to leave them. Real or contrived feelings of indebtedness to the predator may drive kids to do things they would never have done otherwise. For example, the first time victims met the predators in person, 89% of the youth engaged in some form of sex act.[27] Five percent of these children had been sexually abused in the past before the predator attempted to abuse them, and after the abuse began, 16% of the youth survivors were held under duress. In some instances, youth survivors remain with their sex trafficker for a sense of belonging or because the sex trafficker has threatened to harm them or their families.[28] Of

---

[26] Mitchell, K. J., Jones, L. M., Finkelhor, D., & Wolak, J. (2011). Internet-facilitated commercial sexual exploitation of children: Findings from a nationally representative sample of law enforcement agencies in the United States. *Sexual Abuse, 23*(1), 43-71.

[27] Wolak, J., Finkelhor, D., Mitchell, K. J., & Ybarra, M. L. (2010). Online "predators" and their victims: Myths, realities, and implications for prevention and treatment. *American Psychologist, 63*(2), 111-128

[28] Ahern, E. C., Sadler, L. A., Lamb, M. E., & Gariglietti, G. M. (2017). Practitioner perspectives on child sexual exploitation: Rapport building with young people. *Journal of Child Sexual Abuse, 1*, 78.

those solicited online, 25% of the 10 to 13-year-olds were afraid for their lives after they had experienced an aggressive solicitation by a sex predator.[29] Subsequently, traffickers will beat, rape, starve, drug, or isolate their underage survivors from their families and friends to coerce them into submission[30].

---

[29] Mitchell, K. J., Finkelhor, D., & Wolak, J. (2001). Risk factors for and impact of online sexual solicitation of youth. *JAMA: Journal of the American Medical Association, 285*(23), 3011–3014. https://doi-org.stmarys-ca.idm.oclc.org/10.1001/jama.285.23.3011

[30] Kaylor, (2015).

COMMON FLAGS FOR PARENTS AND TEACHERS

For your benefit, I want to share some common flags that parents and teachers should be aware of:

- Children are vulnerable to extra attention. Receiving cash and expensive gifts from an unknown source are common flags for grooming. Children could mask the receipt of gifts by hiding them or claiming they obtained them by legitimate online activities.

- Parents, friends, and teachers can see changes in children's behaviors and attitudes—perhaps anxiousness and fearfulness appear.

- Children begin to have difficulties learning at school and become truant.

- Children spend increasing amounts of time on the Internet and are secretive about their use. Notably, changes in online usage behaviors and secretiveness are signs of problems for your child. For example, they are learning new ways to hide their online activities and social media use.

- Children spend more time with new friends in new social circles than old ones. Importantly, they become cut off from old friends.
- Children detach from family members. They lose interest in their usual activities and hobbies.
- Children change their appearance and dress differently.[31]

More Red Flags for Parents—Interactions You Might Observe

Groomers/predators' online or in-person communications with your child may initially seem low-key. But look and listen carefully; these interactions are often inappropriate or off-kilter. You might feel uneasy seeing or hearing these interactions, but you are unsure why. The tactics can work online or in person, with or without family engagement. Examples include:

- Strangers or newcomers into your lives and/or your children's lives online may come across as very quickly interested or fond of a particular child, among others.
- Although they may be friendly with a family, they typically show more interest in bonding with a specific child than the

---

[31] Nationwide Children's (2011). *Human trafficking: Understanding the red flags.* https://www.nationwidechildrens.org/family-resources-education/700childrens/2017/10/human-trafficking-what-parents-need-to-know

adults. The child becomes their favorite whether in an online social platform, other social circles, or with family.[32] Online, these predators can retain an imposter persona as long as needed to fool children and sometimes parents into believing they are an appropriate friend for their children.

- When parents cannot observe some interactions, the predator must use stealth. These predators begin by subtly stalking a child and looking for opportunities to be alone online or isolated in person.

- Predators can seem over-eager to build trust with the family or the child's online social group and may attempt to integrate themselves with a child's daily life online or in person. If they have physical access and are friendly with the family, they look to be involved in everyday routines and offer help, such as rides to school, help with homework, and tutoring. These opportunities may have been especially easy online during the pandemic. Nevertheless, sometimes, post-pandemic, parents have continued to need help with their kids and appreciate a giving adult.

- The gifts can be given to parents as well as kids

---

[32] Sreenivas, S. (2022).

- Predator patterns include engaging children of a particular age and gender.[33]

Anyone who recognizes the signs described above can reach out to the child with understanding and alert close family members, teachers, friends, and local law enforcement. Help is closer than you think: you can call the National Human Trafficking Hotline at 888-373-7888 or text 233733 anytime, day or night—for free.

Now that you have some insights into who perpetrators are, how they operate, and red flags for you and those in your community, I offer information about family/children-specific risk factors.

Children's and Families' Personal Risk Factors

Many people do not recognize themselves and their children as being among those fitting the profile that predators might seek out. We will start with those most subject to risk and easily identified as targets for predators and move to those less obvious who are nonetheless vulnerable.

A youth who has been physically, sexually, and/or emotionally abused is at a higher risk of becoming a victim. Other factors that raise a youth's vulnerability are an unstable home environment, homelessness, and disputes with their parents/caregivers. Also, if the

---

[33] Sreenivas, S. (2022).

youth victim is having difficulty in school, has been truant at school, or has witnessed or been a survivor of domestic violence, they are at greater risk of being solicited by sex predators. Lastly, if the youth survivor has low self-esteem, has a mental health disorder, and/or uses illicit substances, they are more likely to be solicited.

The most vulnerable sex trafficked populations are young people who are runaways, homeless, in foster care, in poverty, and juvenile delinquent youth.[34] Leaving home is often where the tragedies become full-blown horrors. Parents described to me that after returning home, the physical and mental abuse they suffered. This torture leads to choices parents would never dream their children could make. Some described that their children continued to leave home repeatedly after being found and returned. These patterns are the culmination of effective grooming.

Many of these most susceptible to sex trafficking are children with Adverse Childhood Experiences (ACEs), such as those living with family violence and other forms of domestic violence, poverty, sexual abuse, drug abuse, depression, and other psychological disorders.[35] Children who have experienced life events such as these have life-

---

[34] U.S. Department of Health and Human Services, Family and Youth Services Bureau. (2019). *Human trafficking for runaway and homeless youth serving programs: A resource guide.* https://www.rhyttac.net/assets/docs/Resources/HumanTraffickingResourceGuide-508.pdf

[35] Meeker, E. C., O'Connor, B. C., Kelly, L. M., Hodgeman, D. D., Scheel-Jones, A. H., & Berbary, C. (2021). The impact of adverse childhood experiences on adolescent health risk indicators in a community sample. *Psychological trauma: Theory, research, practice, and policy, 13*(3), 302.

long issues, many of them health-related. The characteristics stand out to traffickers, who look to victimize them at higher rates than other populations.[36]

Among those who have not necessarily acquired ACES status, risks can include substance use, family turmoil, lack of friendships with peers, sexual abuse and early sexual experiences, and young people with diverse gender and sexual identities. Unfortunately, even school system officials can systemically victimize these children.[37] To confound their issues, these survivors and others are often among those in the child welfare and judicial systems.

Notably, due to the pandemic and the rise of child Internet use at home, researchers are finding that the number of at-home youths is increasing and are also at risk. The rising Internet use has created more predation of children from middle and upper-socioeconomic households and those whose parents work long hours and cannot be at home as much. Below are some risks common to those at most risk and those that might appear to be at lower risk. [38]

Substance Abuse. Unfortunately, drug use by young people continues to be widespread. Predators can tap into this vulnerability

---

[36] Kaylor (2015).

[37] National Center on Safe Supportive Learning Environments. (n.d.). *Human trafficking in America's schools. Child sex trafficking.* https://safesupportivelearning.ed.gov/human-trafficking-americas-schools/child-sex-trafficking

[38] Kaylor (2015).

by talking about it and normalizing use. Most importantly, they can become providers of alcohol and drugs. Users have to obtain drugs somehow, and predators can offer a means to create and maintain a drug habit for young people. As mentioned previously, creating drug dependence sets up a secretive relationship between abuser and victim that furthers grooming to move a child or teenager into a sexual relationship and pimp children in human trafficking.

Unsupervised Internet Use. If children can access the Internet within the comfort of their homes without parental monitoring of their electronic devices, they are at higher risk of being solicited online by sex predators[39]. Those with regular, frequent Internet access at home, regardless of family background, are targeted through social media sites, such as Tictok, Facebook, Kik, Craigslist, and Instagram (https://www.parentsagainstchildtrafficking.org/resources).[40] Parents in these situations are often unwitting participants due to work/time constraints and a lack of knowledge about digital devices and social media. Even if parents have restrictions in their homes for Internet, social media, and digital device use, some youths have admitted to accessing the Internet in other people's homes. More discussion

---

[39] Murphy, R. & Fedoroff, J. P. (2014). 10 Legal and Clinical Issues. *Adolescent Sexual Behavior in the Digital Age: Considerations for Clinicians, Legal Professionals, and Educators*, 215.

[40] Parents against child trafficking (2018). *Does your child use these apps?*
https://www.parentsagainstchildtrafficking.org/resources

follows concerning the critical importance of monitoring children's access.

Early Sexualization and Abuse. Many children who are vulnerable to being trafficked have had early age-inappropriate sexual experiences. A 2019 study of 115 underage survivors of sex trafficking found that most of the underage survivors engaged in their first sex act were between the ages of 14-17. Forty-four percent of youth survivors had experienced childhood abuse, 40.9% experienced emotional abuse, and 50% had been raped. Lastly, 35% of youth survivors had a family member involved in the sex industry, and 39.4% knew of a peer who purchased sex before entering the sex industry.[41] Adolescent girls, 14-17 years old, were more likely to be solicited online than boys.[42] In contrast, boys are more susceptible to encountering unwanted sexual solicitation online by male sex predators than girls.[43] These boys sometimes do not report to their parents or authorities because they fear being labeled gay.

Non-conforming Gender and Sexual Identities. Youths identifying as non-conforming gender and sexual identities are at greater risk than many other groups from sexual exploitation and sex

---

[41] Fedina, L., Williamson, C., & Perdue, T. (2019). Risk factors for domestic child sex trafficking in the United States. *Journal of interpersonal violence, 34*(13), 2653-2673.

[42] Mitchell et al. (2001).

[43] Madigan, S., Villani, V., Azzopardi, C., Laut, D., Smith, T., Temple, J. R., & Dimitropoulos, G. (2018). The prevalence of unwanted online sexual exposure and solicitation among youth: A meta-analysis. *Journal of Adolescent Health, 63*(2), 133-141.

trafficking. These young people find identity associated with the LGBTQIA or LGBTQ+ communities (Lesbian, Gay, Bisexual, Transgender, Queer, Intersex, Asexual). These young people often find themselves homeless because their families ask them to leave home due to their orientation and identities. They may also seek contact with whom they believe are LGBTQ+ adults to find validation, community, and sharing. They are more likely to become victims if they cannot find supportive friends and other adults.

SUMMARY AND
ADDITIONAL RISK FACTORS

Be sure to refer to the list often as it summarizes risk factors that you should be aware of:

- History of childhood physical or sexual abuse
- Mental health issues or disorders
- Academically off-track
- Poor self-esteem
- Has run away from home more than once
- Family rejection related to identifying as LGBTQ+
- Lives in a shelter or group home
- Uses drugs or is involved with romantic partners who do
- Family members who have bought sex or been trafficked
- Parents who abuse drugs
- Lives in an area with a large influx of cash-rich workers or tourists
- History of arrests for juvenile status offenses, such as truancy or underage possession of alcohol

Note that unsupervised Internet use is one of the most significant risk factors. This risk is discussed below in the following sections.

Parent-Child Relationships and Prevention

Parents and responsible adults around children need to recognize the challenges your child may face—not just signs of issues after dangerous interactions begin online or otherwise—but also in the milieu of their daily social lives. Current social circumstances are different now than even for parents who also had Internet and social media when younger. Things that came easier for parents in the past have become challenges for kids. As mentioned above, many parents are unaware of their children's contacts through social media apps such as Facebook, Kik, or Instagram. Because online interactions are taking place in our homes, especially busy parents might let it get by us just how much the Internet is changing our world, particularly in the face of unprecedented events like the pandemic. Establishing good communication can be a saving grace before kids get involved with adult strangers—you can learn how to talk to your kids about these challenging topics (https://www.dhs.gov/sites/default/files/

publications/blue_campaign_youth_guide_508_1.pdf; https://preventht.org/programs/parent-resource-center/)[44]

Know that you are not alone in sorting out the best steps to safeguard your children in this complex and hectic world. Parents want to trust their children and believe they would not talk to people they do not know. However, parents' desire to trust is often a myth: children sometimes do not listen to their parents and other adults. Unfortunately, parents are tasked with supporting and supervising their children in ways they may be uncomfortable with and are reluctant to intrude on what they perceive as appropriate freedoms for their children. Studies show that parents checking their children's devices and social media access can lessen young people's chances of exploitation.[45] Parents can feel guilty and conflicted about monitoring children's Internet use because they have provided kids with devices to communicate with harmful strangers. Too much restriction on social media use can isolate children from their healthy social outlets and friends. Finding a balance their children will adhere to is easier said than done; many parents find it challenging to strike the right balance and keep careful watchfulness.

---

[44] Blue Campaign. (n.d.). *How to talk to your kids about human trafficking.* Department of Health and Human Services. https://www.dhs.gov/sites/default/files/publications/blue_campaign_youth_guide_508_1.pdf; Anti-trafficking International. (2022). *Parent Coalition to End Human Trafficking,* https://preventht.org/programs/parent-resource-center/

[45] Brewster (2020).

To ensure their children are not communicating with people unknown to them, first and foremost, families should often talk with their children about the dangers of social media. Resources are available to help you do this, including this book, so your child does not have fear and anxiety after your "talk" with them (https://www.dhs.gov/sites/default/files/publications/blue_campaign_youth_guide_508_1.pdf; https://preventht.org/programs/parent-resource-center/). The key is letting them know you are respecting and keeping them safe.

An effective way to help them stay safe is to enlist them in helping you check their usage and activity. A contract can be valuable; parents and children must sign the contract before the kids receive a device and sign up for specific chat rooms, games, social media platforms, and texting. Make it clear that this is for their safety and well-being. Taking the step alone without engaging them could alienate children and lead to their becoming secretive. Although this is hardly a foolproof step, it is a starting point showing you care. If you must resort to monitoring without their knowledge, just know you are not alone, and sometimes it's necessary.

Specific steps to engaging children could be looking together at their history on phones and computers and storing their passwords on all devices and platforms used. Setting boundaries and checking the histories of these devices can go a long way toward keeping your children safe. However, I consider a multi-tiered approach to monitoring children's devices that can capture activity on many levels. This first example of talking, engaging, and using a contract are some of the most straightforward steps and can be part of a tiered system. Here are more ideas that could be shared with your willing child and some that can be used with kids you suspect are not freely sharing or are turning off functions on their devices.

Given the complexity of devices and online platforms, it's almost mandatory to consider the many levels where their activity is recorded. Conceivably knowledgeable kids can alter their "tracks" without you knowing. However, you can find ways to undo their stealth by monitoring usage if you are vigilant. For example, apps are available to limit children's activity on some sites, particularly social media.

The setting of boundaries can give you both peace of mind. Using a multi-tiered approach, even as savvy as kids can be, may provide you with options they are unaware of or cannot get around. Here is a summary and more detailed steps to ensure their safety and avoid their attempt at stealth if needed.:

- Keep a list of their passwords to all their devices, platforms, and apps. Change them periodically and make them strong.
- Discuss the dangers of Internet and social media use.
- Know what kinds of software and apps are on your child's devices.

- Set up a contract with them, if they are willing, and include many steps to monitor their activity, to which you both consent and should include reconciling their activity in regular meetings with them. For example, look at the browser histories on phones and computers, etc. (see below).

- Educate yourself as well as your children. Potentially, the contract could include that you would use other means if an emergency should arise—you can determine such an emergency without their knowledge if you choose. Also, you might include random checking of devices and usage but make these unplanned.

- Forego a contract and directly monitor social media accounts with or without them, independently of checking their devices.

- Consider limiting texting to known contacts that you approve. Children can quickly get around this one. For example, they might resort to having friends forward texts to them. However, they may be induced to honor the contract if you have other tiers of monitoring them and they know it.

- Go straight to the devices and companies that produce/sell them for help and information: Apple offers family-sharing device settings for children to limit screen time and block purchases. However, keeping kids safe takes far more than limiting the time and money they might use. Apple and

Android phones offer many other lines of defense. Information about these is readily available online; see below.

- You can have two or more phones on a single account besides a shared family account (e.g., Apple has this feature). These phones can be synced to share text messages that appear on both phones. However, you will have less privacy because your messages will also show on the child's phone. Alternatively, you can have a third phone linked to the account and receive the child's messages but not yours. You could consider checking this phone with or without your child's knowledge.

- Go to your cell phone service provider accounts. This one can be *very effective* as you do not necessarily want to share your password for a billing account. Call records and text content from some companies, such as Verizon, can be retrieved. Children may not know how much information you can get— you can link the time and source of a text to those stored in their phone history. If some are missing from their phone, then you will know. This strategy could deter children from turning off phone settings when using Apple or Android account sharing. If necessary, this can be used without their knowledge.

- Apps are made for Android phones that forward text messages to a computer. While teenagers will likely object, an agreement to look together and ignore messages from their known contacts might suffice.

- A family sharing plan on Apple or Android devices is like sharing one account. These backup text messages and pictures to your joint cloud space if they are not quickly deleted or the phone sharing to the cloud remains disabled.

- Set up regular backups of your child's computer to a cloud platform. Do not give them the password; tell them you will know if the regular backup is skipped.

- Keeping the passwords to yourself for joint phone cloud accounts or family sharing can deter them from removing activity, but they find ways to turn off backup functions and/or erase them before backup. There are software apps that can recover messages in some cases.

- Microsoft and other companies can give you the means to prevent kids from erasing the history on their Window-driven computers and devices (Appendix).[46] Find out what Apple may have for Mac computers and iPads.[47] If you use PCs and phones other than Apple, check with other companies that offer other PCs.

---

[46] Microsoft. *How to stop my child for clearing his browser.* https://answers.microsoft.com/en-us/windows/forum/all/how-to-stop-my-child-from-clearing-his-browsing/c73f6f12-19ed-40e7-80e3-704436a275a9

[47] Apple. *Expanded protection for children.* https://www.apple.com/child-safety/

- Restrict which browsers your child uses so they cannot easily hide Internet activity on a browser unknown to you—block installation of new browsers and then monitor activity. For example, Google allows joint accounts for email on Chrome; you could link your account to your child's and ensure that your child's accounts are all linked. Google also allows periodic downloads of activity on browsers and email activity. When you collect their activity, watch out for email accounts you do not know about. Social media accounts might be a good location to check for additional email accounts they have created, and some information will be in their browser histories.

- Do not allow your child to have cloud services for backup you do not know about; for example, Windows One Drive could store information removed from a computer hard drive. And One Drive comes free and is installed on most Windows computers.

- As mentioned above, many apps can be installed on children's phones and your phone or computer that allow monitoring activities. Location and tracking movement services can be especially valuable. Again, search the Internet; these will not be hard to find.

While checking activity is one of the more difficult decisions, parents are likely unaware of how valuable this can be. This topic is expanded below with parent education and the impacts of monitoring. These steps are challenging and time-consuming, but keeping them safe is worth it.

The Importance of Monitoring Children's Internet and Digital Communications

The value of parental monitoring of youth Internet use is well-supported by researchers.[48] A lack of parental monitoring is a critical risk factor regarding solicitation by online sex predators. The risk factors are discussed at length in this book, and I encourage parents to use the resources in the appendix and seek out other sources on the Internet, in the community, with teachers, school administrators, and mental health professionals regarding monitoring use and risks.

Despite the discomfort and difficulties of tracking youths' use of the devices, the Internet, and social media, parents, teachers, and the school community should understand just how valuable and practical it can be. In a study of parental monitoring of their children's use of digital technologies and the Internet, 66% of parents reported that they frequently monitor their children's Internet use; however, when kids were asked the same question, only 38% reported that their parents monitored their Internet use regularly.[49] About half of these

---

[48]Reid, J., & Fox, B. (2020).

[49] Wang, R., Bianchi, S. M., & Raley, S. B. (2005). Teenagers' Internet use and family rules: A

parents believed they had rules regarding their children's Internet usage, but again, in contrast, their children reported that no rules existed in their families or that they only had rules about their length of use. Sixty-six percent of these youths' parents also reported that their children knew more about the Internet and digital devices than they did[50].

Parents of teens are less likely to monitor their teenager's Internet use or place monitoring software on their devices. Parents over 40 years old and with a high school diploma were less likely to monitor their youth's Internet usage versus a parent younger than 40 and with a college education. Furthermore, the study identified that fathers monitored their youth's electronic devices more frequently than mothers. Lastly, the study found that parents who shared a computer with their children monitored their Internet browsing history and set boundaries, which decreased the risk of their children talking to unknown sex predators or being solicited online.[51]

research note. *Journal of Marriage and Family*, *67*(5), 1249-1258.

[50] Wang et al. (2015)

[51] Wang et al. (2015)

NAVIGATE
ASSISTANCE SYSTEMS

To help people understand the problem, let's begin with understanding some aspects of the legal system you might encounter in the worst-case scenario—sex trafficking. To understand the legal supports, we can start with the legal definitions of sex trafficking and the laws in place.

Law enforcement personnel and the judicial system consider sex trafficking as recruiting, sheltering, transporting, furnishing, or acquiring people to participate in for-profit sex. While all sex trafficking is illegal, if the target is under 18, no acts of coercion or force need to be a part of activities in arrests for breaking these laws.[52] The problem of sexually abusing kids does not exclude non-commercial kidnapping and sexual abuse of children through online communication with strangers or even known individuals. According to federal law, youth who are under the age of 18 are unable to

---

[52] Litham, 2017

consent to sex[53]. In conjunction with lawmakers, resources and national networks have been established.

National Center for Missing and Exploited Children and Legal Safeguards

In 1984, the National Center for Missing and Exploited Children was established after a 6-year-old boy, Adam Walsh, was kidnapped from a mall in Florida by a sex offender.[54] The agency supports families, advocates, and law enforcement regarding missing and sexually exploited children. The National Center for Missing and Exploited Children's mission was to disseminate information about trafficked youth to state, federal, and international law enforcement agencies to deter predators from crossing state or international borders. In 1984, Congress also enacted The Missing Children Act, which provided funding for the Office of Justice programs to aid local, state, and federal agencies in locating and returning missing children.[55] Adam Walsh's father, John Walsh, assisted Congress in creating a 24-hour crisis/tip hotline to inform law enforcement and parents about missing children and reunify them with their parents.[56]

---

[53] Kaylor 2015.

[54] Murder of Adam Walsh. (2023, June 22). In *Wikipedia*. https://en.wikipedia.org/wiki/Murder_of_Adam_Walsh

[55] U.S. Department of Justice. (!984). Missing Children Act. Office of Justice Programs. *FBI Law Enforcement Bulletin, 53*(1), 17-20.

[56] Milian, J. (2019, March 14). *America's Most Wanted" host John Walsh helps unveil call center.*

In 1998, the National Center for Missing and Exploited Children extended the information pipeline with the CyberTipline for anyone to report online solicitation of a child through the Internet in chatrooms, emails, or social media sites; the tip line is not limited to child pornography.[57] The National Center for Missing and Exploited Children website (https://www.missingkids.org) can receive anonymous reports 24 hours a day of suspected child abuse, sexual exploitation, or online solicitation through electronic devices.

During the early 2000s, several other federal laws were put into place to protect children under 18 from various contexts of sexual abuse. For example, The Trafficking Victims Protection Act (TVPA) protects survivors, supports prosecuting predators, and prevents trafficking locally, statewide, and internationally. Sex traffickers found guilty under the TVPA could receive life sentences. With the growing use of the Internet, sex traffickers have been able to solicit, recruit, control, and exploit more victims without being apprehended by law enforcement.[58]

Congress and the public have recognized the differences in how online predators of children can operate. Therefore, additional legislation in the form of a reauthorized TVPA was enacted to

---

for missing, exploited children. The Palm Beach Post.

[57] Detrick, S. (1998).

[58] Prylinski, K. M. (2020). Tech trafficking: How the Internet has transformed sex trafficking. *Journal of High Technology Law, 20,* 338.

---

address predators' methods comprehensively. Laws and sentences such as this have shored up the justice system in ensuring that perpetrators cannot victimize children again. The PROTECT Act is another significant step forward for prevention that parents and schools should be aware of. This act established America's Missing: Broadcast Emergency Response (AMBER) Alert System. The system is named after Amber Hagerman, a 9-year-old girl abducted in Texas while riding her bicycle.[59] The AMBER Alert was established to help disseminate information on abducted or missing children to law enforcement agencies and communities immediately upon reporting a missing child.[60]

The resources available through the local systems can vary greatly. For example, in some rural communities, there are limited resources for youth survivors, so they often detain survivors in a juvenile hall detention facility or place them in a group home to keep them safe. However, this experience can re-traumatize the survivors. Parents are encouraged to learn as much as they can about national and local supports.

---

[59] Rogers, A. (2009). Protecting children on the Internet: Mission impossible. *Baylor Law Review, 61,* 323.
[60] Zgoba, K. (2004). The Amber Alert: The appropriate solution to preventing child abduction?. *The Journal of Psychiatry & Law, 32*(1), 71-88.

Trauma, Consequences, and Outcomes

Young people who have been sex trafficked by predators experience an array of physical symptoms associated with sexual exploitation; these include inflammatory illness, sexually transmitted infections, HIV/AIDS, unsafe abortions, pelvic discomfort, headaches, dizziness, and physical injuries, which include broken bones, a black eye, and/or bruises.[61] Ottisova and colleagues described some physical consequences youths experience at the hands of their perpetrators: sexually transmitted diseases, pregnancy, physical injuries, drug misuse, and starvation.[62]Youth survivors may also experience psychological impacts such as difficulties trusting friends and family, volatile family and peer relationships, anger management issues, anxiety, and posttraumatic stress disorder (PTSD). In addition, youth survivors experience nightmares, insomnia, anxiety, depression, and panic disorders.[63] Youth sex trafficking survivors can be at a higher risk of using alcohol and drugs than survivors of other forms of trafficking, such as non-sexual human trafficking and forced labor, and need substance abuse care.

---

[61] Volgin, R. N., Shakespeare-Finch, J., & Shochet, I. M. (2019). Posttraumatic distress, hope, and growth in survivors of commercial sexual exploitation in Nepal. *Traumatology, 25*(3), 181.
[62] Ottisova, L., Smith, P., Shetty, H., Stahl, D., Downs, J., & Oram, S. (2018). Psychological consequences of child trafficking: An historical cohort study of trafficked children in contact with secondary mental health services. *PLoS one, 13*(3), e0192321.
[63] Volgin et al. (2019).

When predator these encounters occur during a child's formative years, the negative consequences can be long-lasting and tragic. In severe circumstances, children who have been sexually exploited exhibit symptoms comparable to those of torture victims.[64] Many child survivors of sex trafficking frequently engage in self-harm and suicidality. Lastly, sex-trafficked survivors have difficulty setting boundaries and developing healthy relationships with others. [65]

Supporting and Educating Parents, the Community, and the Public

Knowledge is power. My goal of educating parents and other stakeholders stems from my time as a corrections officer in Oakland, CA. As a 22-year veteran Deputy Probation Officer, I witnessed the horror of parents, caregivers, teachers, and other responsible adults, and most unfortunately, the pain of children and young people. I state the dire consequences I saw again because it is too easy to overlook the warning signs, especially when our children are in the care of others, such as school officials and even at home. In my work, I learned first-hand how victimized youths became connected to people online whom they knew little about—they were essentially strangers. In addition to working with local law enforcement, schools,

---

[64] Volgin et al. (2019).
[65] Levine, J. A. (2017). Mental health issues in survivors of sex trafficking. *Cogent Medicine*, *4*(1), 1278841; Ottisova et al. (2018).

and mental health organizations, we can all come together as a community to provide ongoing dialogue and interventions.

Interventions That Can Start Healing and Therapeutic Approaches

Before moving on to more intensive therapy approaches, I would like to introduce some interventions and resources available to child survivors that contribute to healing and the therapeutic process. Many resources and interventions emphasize building rapport with survivors.[66] This process alone can have therapeutic value for abuse survivors, particularly child trafficking survivors. Beginning the process of trust is of the utmost, given the shame and repressed pain that can be instilled in them. Community services can aim to help these children open up and maybe ready themselves for more intensive help and the life changes that come with it. Additionally, kids with no home or not welcomed by their families could have a lifeline for survival while they find ways to obtain medical and psychological help. Parents benefit from knowing their children receive support outside the home and within a welcoming community.

Survivors like these lack trust and feel guilty about what happened to them. They are reluctant to accept help; however, community

---

[66] Ahern, E. C., Sadler, L. A., Lamb, M. E., & Gariglietti, G. M. (2017). Practitioner perspectives on child sexual exploitation: Rapport building with young people. *Journal of Child Sexual Abuse, 1,* 78.

resources that offer confidentiality between children and trained adults can bridge the way forward. Especially for runaways, someplace to recuperate that meets their basic needs could encourage them to seek more help.[67] Although these children will likely fear authority figures. an accessible environment where little is asked of them can help.

I believe it is vital for parents and kids to learn about the various interventions and types of abuse. Using help from professionals can help parents effectively support their victimized children. A description of some consequences and specific interventions follows in this section.

---

[67] US Department of Health and Human Services (2019).
https://www.rhyttac.net/assets/docs/Resources/HumanTraffickingResourceGuide-508.pdf

FAMILY AND COMMUNITY SUPPORT

Individual, family, peer, school, and community interventions could be combined into traditional therapy, including parent training and skill development. Notably, some child survivors of commercial sexual exploitations have little or no contact with their biological families; dysfunctional family systems are key risk factors for survivorization.[68] If available, a survivor's biological or non-biological family members should be included in the healing process.

Researchers have suggested that homeless and runaway kids' risks of sex trafficking are reduced if homeless shelters and drop-in centers are accessible. For example, drop-in centers can offer safety and reduce ongoing harm. The services can include drug abuse prevention and sexual health promotion. Youth drop-in centers and homeless shelters frequently offer case management and emergency supplies, such as food, blankets, showers, and personal hygiene

---

[68] O'Brien et al. (2022).

goods.[69] These centers are shown to work! Kids who use them have fewer days on the run, out of school, mental health problems, and incidents of substance abuse.

In another example that includes sexual health, girls who received HIV education through the "Street Smart" program engage less often in unprotected sex than those who received no education. Sexual health interventions, such as abstinence, safe sex, and condoms, help reduce the risk of sexually transmitted infections; these interventions are also recommended for survivors of sex trafficking.[70]

Lastly, kinship care can be an excellent alternative to traditional foster care or residential treatment for youth who cannot go to their immediate families. Apart from their nuclear families, these young people can often be with extended family members in kinship care. The benefits are similar to drop-in and homeless centers, but these kids in kinship care experience many benefits, such as fewer behavioral problems, mental health illnesses, and a greater sense of well-being than those in non-kinship foster care. Some advantages of kinship care include eventual family reunions and fewer runaways.[71] The examples I offer here do not include everything available, so review the resource list in the appendix.

---

[69] O'Brien et al. (2022).

[70] Rotheram-Borus, M. J., Song, J., Gwadz, M., Lee, M., Rossem, R. V., & Koopman, C. (2003). Reductions in HIV risk among runaway youth. *Prevention Science, 4*(3), 173-187.

[71] O'Brien et al. (2022).

Substance Abuse Intervention and Resources. Because many predators gain control of their targets using drugs or alcohol, O'Brien and colleagues suggested an initial intervention should be a treatment for substance abuse, either out or inpatient.[72] These abuse programs should include family engagement and support. Young people can succeed more often in drug and alcohol programs if family members join the support team. Supportive parents and family can help decrease resistance to changing children's daily habits, such as spending much time online. Maintaining old triggers for substance abuse, such as excessive online time, interferes with their progress. Group therapy for substance and sexual abuse is known to be effective for young people. We can expect that these therapies could be helpful for kids and parents to let go of the shame and fear associated with sex trafficking. We all need to know we are not alone.

---

[72] O'Brien et al. (2022).

MENTORING SERVICES

Similar to the support received from various group therapies, a second intervention proposed is one-on-one mentors. Like alcohol and drug abuse sponsors, mentors for sex trafficking victims can meet with young people for support and in emergencies. Some can also provide academic tutoring to help them catch up with school.[73] Individual and group therapy mentors can help these survivors avoid delinquency and return to their prior lifestyle. If they relapse with destructive behaviors, they might fear punishment if it is brought to light. Mentors, parents, and professionals must emphasize that these children can tell the truth.

Why Pursue Therapy?

I believe it is vital for you and your child to learn about the more intensive interventions and therapies that can benefit you. In doing so, parents can make the best choice of therapy for their children. If a child suffering the repercussions of sex solicitation and trafficking

---

[73] O'Brien et al. (2022).

receives treatment as early as possible, the chances for steady recovery increase. Using help from professionals, parents can more effectively support their victimized children. Parents experience trauma, as well as their children, after heinous events. As many say, self-care is essential, but you must help yourself to help others.

A growing body of evidence *suggests* that, similar to many types of trauma survivors, therapy can be critical to survivorship and recovery.[74] Few, if any, therapeutic approaches are tailored specifically to sex trafficking survivors, but as mentioned above, similar techniques as those for sexual abuse survivors and other forms of abuse likely transfer well to sex trafficking survivors.[75] For example, PTSD occurs for almost all survivors of various traumatic events, and the methods used to help them will most likely help survivors of sex traffickers. Note to parents: consider your child's symptoms and the various types of treatment available in your vicinity. Because little evidence exists for showing the most effective approaches to survivors of sex trafficking, you should consider the various types and ask yourself: what kind of therapy will fit my child's needs, and in what setting should my child's treatment proceed?

---

[74] O'Brien et al. (2022).

[75] Ahern, E. C., Sadler, L. A., Lamb, M. E., & Gariglietti, G. M. (2017). Practitioner perspectives on child sexual exploitation: Rapport building with young people. *Journal of Child Sexual Abuse, 1*, 78

A key question you may have is, why don't some people seek treatment after these horrible experiences related to sex trafficking? Among other reasons, young people solicited and/or trafficked often distrust law enforcement and medical professionals and are often unwilling to share their stories.[76] Parents may feel shame that they did not protect and intervene more quickly. Some of these reasons are shame-based and present a complex psychological rationale challenging for individuals to overcome.

Others avoid therapy because they minimize the effects of abuse and trauma. Some of us might assume that online sex trafficking is less distressing for survivors if it does not lead to some of the more harmful outcomes, such as face-to-face sexual abuse and drug addiction. However, parents need to know that even less invasive interactions with predators' and their controlling forms of grooming can traumatize kids in persisting ways, such as a lack of trust and difficulties in relationships. Note that even if predators' actions largely did not succeed with a target, the manipulation kids experienced through grooming can mar a child's perceptions of the world. Regardless of the level of exposure a child has to sexual predators and trafficking, you, as a parent, should consider the benefits of psychological treatment for your child. Below, I describe a

---

[76] Scarafia, R. M. (2014). Human trafficking: The need for stronger legislation in Louisiana to protect victims. *Loyola Law Review, 60*, 687.

form of therapy that, after researching, I can endorse as a basis for interventions.

What is Narrative Therapy?

As I learned more about sex trafficking and its repercussions, I gravitated to Narrative Therapy. Narrative Therapy has guided my understanding of children facing online predators and potential sex trafficking. I found it consistent with meeting the needs of these children. Michael White and David Epston defined Narrative Therapy as a process of "storying" and/or "re-storying" our lives and experiences to benefit an understanding of our realities.[77] These investigators considered that individuals could build personal narratives about life events and experiences and come to conclusions about themselves and their identities.[78] They propose that participants build upon or construct a new meaning of life through interpretive stories that they can treat as truths. Narrative Therapy is a collaborative effort between the client(s) and the therapist. The strategies work from the strengths of individuals while not characterizing participants as unhealthy or abnormal. Children,

---

[77] Baştemur, Ş., & Baş, E. (2021). Integration of narrative therapy with expressive art practices. *Current Approaches in Psychiatry, 13*(1), 146–169. https://doi-org.stmarys-ca.idm.oclc.org/10.18863/pgy.771319; White, M. (2007). *Maps of narrative practice.* W. W. Norton & Co.

[78] Bastemur, S., & Baş, E. (2021); Corey, G. (2016). *Theory and practice of group counseling* (9th ed.). Brooks/Cole-Thomson Learning.

parents, and other adults' emotional reactions to these horrific stories are typical for those genuinely caring for others; however, the expression of these reactions should be focused on survivors' strengths. This therapy is an empowering approach that emphasizes eliminating self-blame.

When a person internalizes a tale consisting of a limited or unfavorable description of themselves that lacks positive self-regard, emotional pain, and coping problems arise. White and Epston believe that when such a tale becomes the dominant narrative in a person's life, it limits their self-concept, causing them to overlook the positives about themselves. Internalizing and accepting a negative story as reality reinforces emotional and cognitive problems rather than healing.[79]

Narrative Therapy also aims to unearth and promote positive and preferred identity stories from the client and assist clients in re-storying. In the next step, participants are encouraged to separate their past sense of identity from a current problem and re-story their capacity as "fighting back." The positive aspects of clients' self-perceptions in their stories can be used in the future to support coping with new or related life events. Rather than attempting to modify or change the individual, Narrative Therapy focuses on transforming the

---

[79] Bastemur, S. & & Baş, E., (2021); White (2007).

problem's impact. Narrative Therapy focuses on a non-blaming stance that includes compassion and guides young people to become experts in their lives. Feelings of self-efficacy from self-regulation and agency open them up to sharing with professionals and others who can help. These strategies focus on individuals' resilience and skills to mitigate life difficulties.[80] I present aspects of a pilot program that utilizes this form of therapy in the sections below.

The Tree of Life. The Tree of Life technique is designed to help children communicate traumatic experiences in ways that can strengthen them. Children are encouraged to create their own "Tree of Life" to identify where they came from, their ambitions and dreams, and the essential people in their lives. They also identify negative influences and talk about their traumatic experience without judgment and blame while strengthening their connections with themselves, their community, and family.[81] As mentioned above, the program I suggest for children who were sex trafficked is a narrative approach incorporating the Tree of Life techniques.

A takeaway from this book is that to combat online sex trafficking, parents and youth must be aware of the dangers of social media. Parents must educate themselves and their children on the dangers of

---

[80] White, M. (2007).
[81] White, M. (2011). *Narrative practice: Continuing the conversations.* W W. Norton & Co.

the Internet. Parental actions should include setting boundaries and randomly checking their kids' electronic devices. The parent must know their children's password to all their electronic devices, including gaming units. If a youth is at risk of being sex trafficked or has been trafficked, parents should seek out therapy that they have investigated and fits their child. Overcoming trauma from sex trafficking requires multiple sources of support.

Given that many sex predators isolate their young victims from their families and communities, family members of trafficked youth should work to remain closely connected with their kids. Furthermore, families of sex trafficked survivors should also be included in their children's recovery process. I next outline a treatment program based on what I have learned and am in the process of developing.

RECLAIMING OUR LIVES: HEALING IS POSSIBLE

My drive to understand the problem of child sex trafficking led me to think deeply about the healing process for survivors and the kinds of support groups that benefit them. A support group I would endorse allows survivors privacy and a chance to share their experiences and feelings with other survivors, gain coping strategies, and learn about community resources.

My vision of such a support group is a 9-week program for young people targeted by sex trafficking predators: The Reclaiming Our Lives program. The program is founded in Narrative Therapy and the Tree-of-Life approach and takes place in a safe, non-judgmental group format. Program participants are counseled using the dynamics of a group setting and encouraged to discuss their trauma freely. In this format, the survivors can acknowledge that they are not alone. The process follows the Tree of Life strategy, where participants metaphorically identify aspects of their lives using a tree representing their past, present, and future.[82] This concrete example of their life paths allows them to develop a victim-to-survivor mental shift, as proscribed in a Narrative Therapy setting. During the program, the participants learn about available resources and receive support. The survivors develop competencies to transfer the blame of the sex-trafficked experience from themselves to the perpetrators. A goal for the group is to support survivors in gaining trust, developing self-esteem, improving community connections, reducing shame, and learning how to set physical and emotional boundaries.

---

[82] White, M., (2011).

CONCLUSION

Takeaways from this book are that to combat online sex trafficking, parents and youth must be aware of the dangers of social media. Parents must educate themselves and their children on the dangers of the Internet. Parental actions should include setting boundaries and randomly checking their kids' electronic devices. The parent must know their children's password to all their electronic devices, including gaming units. Information is available to educate and support parents in taking these steps. Understanding the warning signs and outcomes is critical for the prevention efforts of parents and schools. If a youth is at risk of being sex trafficked or has been trafficked, parents should seek out therapy that they have investigated and fits their child. Overcoming trauma from sex trafficking requires multiple sources of support. The significant growth of sex trafficking begs the question: why are there not more face-to-face and accessible resources in local communities?

AFTERWORD

Thank you for purchasing and reading my book. I am encouraged and grateful to know that others may be helped through this book. As I described, my passion for this topic began when I worked as a probation officer. I was supervising minors who were commercially and sexually trafficked throughout the Bay Area. During supervision, I noticed that this at-risk population's new "pimp" was social media, cell phones, iPads, laptops, and gaming units. Many parents were unaware of this new phenomenon. When some parents realized their youths had been conversing with strangers, it was too late to prevent significant harm. I have witnessed youth turn against their parents because the sex predator had groomed them to believe their parents do not love them. I have also seen youths becoming exposed to drugs, physical/emotional abuse, and unwanted pregnancy at the hands of their predators. One of the most complex parts of being a Deputy Probation Officer was listening to parents say, "How do I get my child back from that monster." Unfortunately, I could not answer that question for them, and it haunted me.

What I want you to know: Parents often hand their children a key to an unknown world without setting boundaries, monitoring activity by knowing passwords, or having conversations about sex and strangers. Please understand that predators could also be people they know, which is even more dangerous! As parents, we prioritize keeping our children safe from themselves and others; however, many fail to protect them because we lack knowledge. This book became my first promise to the sex-trafficked youth that I could not protect as a Deputy Probation Officer. I promised to educate parents on the importance of checking and monitoring their youngsters' electronic devices. Parents must converse with their youth about sex, boundaries, and social media before providing a child with an electronic device.

Furthermore, parents must remind the youth that they will periodically monitor their social media sites, read their text messages, and listen to them play their gaming unit for their safety. The youth should understand that the parent does trust them; however, the parent does not trust who is on the other side of that device. Parents, we must promise our youth that we will check their devices frequently to keep them safe! Our youth must commit to "Don't Chat Back" with unknown strangers.

RESOURCES

Examples of software and phone provider advice:

Microsoft advice and instructions on monitoring your children's internet use: https://answers.microsoft.com/en-us/windows/forum/all/how-to-stop-my-child-from-clearing-his-browsing/c73f6f12-19ed-40e7-80e3-704436a275a9

Apple suggestions as a starting point for parents: https://www.apple.com/child-safety/

These examples are just two of many to be found online, including advice from Android makers. Also, look for advice online from search engine companies such as Google and Foxfire.

Social media platforms such as Facebook also publish advice online.

Online immediate and comprehensive resources:

The National Center for Missing and Exploited Children's database, https://www.missingkids.org/

National Human Trafficking Resource Center, 24-hour national help, 1-888-373-7888 or text 233733.

Love146 is a comprehensive source and program description https://love146.org/resources/#:~:text=Reach%20out%20to%20the%20National,to%20find%20resources%20and%20help.

Anti-trafficking International. (2022). *Parent Coalition to End Human Trafficking,* https://preventht.org/programs/parent-resource-center/

STAND! For Families Free of Violence provides support and shelter for trafficked youth, 24-Hour Crisis Line 1-888-215-5555, Fax: 925-676-0274, Email: crisisline@standffov.org, https://www.standffov.org

Community Violence Solution (CVS) provides crisis response and case management services to victims of sex trafficking, 24/7 crisis line at 1-800-670-7273 or text "CVS" to 20121, https://cvsolutions.org

MISSEY

Motivating. Inspiring, Supporting, and Serving Sexually Exploited Youth

The program is located at 424 Jefferson Street, Oakland, CA 94607, 510-251-2070, www.missey.org

The program offers case management services and resources to youth who are at risk of being sex trafficked and have been sex trafficked.

BAWAR's (Bay Area Women Against Rape)

The program is located at 470 27th Street, Oakland, CA 94612, 24/7 hotline (510) 345-1056, www.bawar.org BAWAR offers 24-hour crisis response, individual peer counseling, advocacy, and court accompaniments.

Contra Costa County Family Justice Centers provide services to families affected by sex trafficking, domestic violence, and sexual assault. Concord 925-521-6366, Richmond 510-974-2200, Antioch 925-281-0970.

Some fact sheets with definitions and statistics concerning sex trafficking:

Polaris Project. (2019). *Child trafficking and the child welfare system.* Polaris Project. https://polarisproject.org/wp-content/uploads/2019/09/Child-Welfare-Fact-Sheet.pdf;

NCAI Policy Research Center. (2016). *Human & sex trafficking: Trends and responses across Indian country. Tribal Insights Brief.* NCAI Policy Research Center. https://www.ncai.org/policy-research-center/research-data/prc-publications/TraffickingBrief.pdf;

National Center for Missing and Exploited Children. (2020). *Child sex trafficking identification resource.* National Center for Missing and Exploited Children. https://www.missingkids.org/content/dam/missingkids/pdfs/CST%20Identification%20Resource.pdf

U.S. Department of Health and Human Services, Family and Youth Services Bureau. (2019). *Human trafficking for runaway and homeless youth serving programs: A resource guide.* https://www.rhyttac.net/assets/docs/Resources/HumanTraffickingResourceGuide-508.pdf

U.S. Department of Health and Human Services, Administration for Children and Families. https://www.acf.hhs.gov/sites/default/files/documents/cb/report_congress_child_trafficking.pdf

A government resource page provides more information on sponsored resources and laws that govern child sex trafficking:

U.S. Department of Health and Human Welfare. Children's Bureau of Resources. Child Trafficking.

https://www.childwelfare.gov/topics/systemwide/trafficking/acfresources/cbresources/

A compendium of resources and information from Parents Against Child Trafficking:

Parents against child trafficking (2018). *Does your child use these apps?* https://www.parentsagainstchildtrafficking.org/resources

Parent Organization:

Anti-trafficking International. (2022). *Parent Coalition to End Human Trafficking,* https://preventht.org/programs/parent-resource-center/

Nationwide Children's (2011). *Human trafficking: Understanding the red flags.* https://www.nationwidechildrens.org/family-resources-education/700childrens/2017/10/human-trafficking-what-parents-need-to-know

Information for Schools, Teachers, and Parents

National Center on Safe Supportive Learning Environments Human Trafficking in America's Information for Schools Child Sex Trafficking https://safesupportivelearning.ed.gov/human-trafficking-americas-schools/child-sex-trafficking

This site has links on various topics, including risks and vulnerable populations. See the links below.

- Child Sex Trafficking
- Trafficking is Child Abuse
- Vulnerable Populations
- Risk Factors
- Indicators
- Trafficking in Urban, Suburban, and Rural Areas
- Impact on the Students and the Learning Environment
- Preventing Child Trafficking at the School Level
- Community Partnerships
- School Policies and Protocols to Combat Trafficking
- Resources and Support
- Terms and Definitions
- Full Guide (PDF)

www.ingramcontent.com/pod-product-compliance
Lightning Source LLC
Chambersburg PA
CBHW022123170526
45157CB00004B/1733